April 2016

Body Painting

for Sunnie,
who makes me
beautiful, and
for Dean
who makes
Sunnie happy ～

with love,
Jane

# Body Painting

Poems

J ANE  H ILBERRY

Red Hen Press   Los Angeles

*Body Painting*

Cover images:
    Photography by Christoper Voelker, © 2005 by Christoper Voelker
    Body painting by Melanie Manson and Eli Crawford

Book design by Michael Vukadinovich
Cover Design by Mark E. Cull

ISBN: 1-59709-013-1
Library of Congress Catalog Card Number: 2004117567

Published by Red Hen Press

The City of Los Angeles Cultural Affairs Department, California Arts Council, Los Angeles County Arts Commission and National Endowment for the Arts partially support Red Hen Press.

First Edition

# Acknowledgments

Thanks to the editors of the magazines in which the following poems previously appeared, sometimes in different versions:

Calyx: "Crazy Jane Goes to Painting Class." Reprinted in *Fierce Brightness: Twenty-Five Years of Women's Poetry*. Calyx Books, 2002; *Denver Quarterly Review*: "The Visitation"; *Eleventh Muse*: "Joy" (published as "A Shell, for a Friend Who Lives by the Sea"); *Flyway*: "Hush," "Radish"; *Grrrrr: A Collection of Poems about Bears*, Arctos Press: "Crazy Jane Meets a Bear"; *High Plains Literary Review*: "Fireweed"; *Hudson Review*: "The Car Salesman," "The Moment"; *Inhabiting the Body: A Collection of Poetry and Art by Women*. Moon Journal Press, 2002: "Elegant"; *The Journal*: "Sand"; *Lake Effect*: "Crazy Jane Sleeps on Page C of the Logician's Dictionary" and "We Say"; *Many Mountains Moving*: "Crazy Jane Defaults on Her Loan"; *Michigan Quarterly Review*: "Relativity"; *Mid-American Review*: "Crazy Jane Talks with Bones"; *Virginia Quarterly Review*: "Train"; *Women's Review of Books*: "Blizzard" and "In Arabic"

A number of these poems appeared in a chapbook titled *The Girl with the Pearl Earring*, published originally by The Press at Colorado College (1989) and reprinted by JonesAlley Press (1995).

My thanks to Colorado College for a Benezet Grant, a Jackson Fellowship, and many hours of release time which allowed me to work on these poems. Thanks also to the Colorado Council on the Arts and the Ragdale Foundation.

I have received advice and support from more people than I can acknowledge. You know who you are! I want especially to thank my Colorado Springs community, Diane, Mary Lou, Lynn, Larry, David and Dick; my English Department friends & colleagues; the members of What Would Lorca Do?; my teachers Roger Mitchell and Ellen Bryant Voigt; Jim Moore; Kate Holaday; and, with love, my parents Conrad and Marion Hilberry and my sisters Marilyn Day and Ann Hilberry.

My apologies to Yeats.

# Contents

## I

| | |
|---|---|
| Ave Maria | 15 |
| The Car Salesman | 16 |
| Crazy Jane Meets a Bear | 18 |
| The Driver | 19 |
| Crazy Jane Sleeps on Page C of the Logician's Dictionary | 20 |
| Expert | 21 |
| Fireweed | 22 |
| Crazy Jane: Nothing Personal | 23 |
| Crazy Jane Defaults on Her Loan | 24 |
| She Keeps Her Heart | 25 |
| The Visitation | 26 |
| You Are Here | 27 |
| Total Immersion | 28 |
| The Mineral of Skin | 30 |

## II

| | |
|---|---|
| Listening | 35 |
| The Silence | 36 |
| In Arabic | 37 |
| Elegant | 38 |
| Crazy Jane Talks with Bones | 39 |
| Pioneer | 40 |
| Radish | 41 |
| Crazy Jane Goes to Painting Class | 42 |
| Relativity | 43 |
| Epithalamion | 44 |
| Train | 45 |
| Weeding the Cosmos | 46 |

## III

| | |
|---|---|
| Ocean | 49 |
| Joy | 50 |
| Questions | 51 |
| She | 52 |
| Crazy Jane: Alike in This | 53 |
| Body Painting | 54 |
| Train Whistle | 55 |
| Swaying | 56 |
| My Mother's Beauty | 57 |
| The Moment | 59 |
| Things to Do | 60 |
| Conception: Dialogues with Several Children and a Cosmologer | 61 |
| Hush | 64 |
| Blizzard | 66 |
| Sand | 67 |
| We Say | 68 |

Body Painting

# I.

Have you ever loved the Body of a woman?
Have you ever loved the Body of a man?

—Walt Whitman

## Ave Maria

I had a lover once, a good poet, funny,
but I didn't want to take his body
into mine. Only occasionally did I go
to the lesbian bar, where suddenly my energy
was as large as the room, as loud
as the music that pulsed under the ticking,
glittering globe above.

I've had two women lovers,
one named Eva, the other Maria.
From their names, a phrase
about which masses have been sung.
Right now, one of my students is pregnant,
will have an abortion. I look at her,
perfect girth of her hips, and I want
to tell her *don't send this spirit away*—
imagine Mary telling Gabriel
*no, I'm sorry, I'm busy now,
it's not convenient.*

All those years I kept
trading in men, thinking it might
happen to me: husband, child, a line
I could draw around myself and say
*family.* The angel came to me,
*Ave Maria,* and I sent him away, saying
*I need Joseph and a couple of mules.*
I sent him away, when everything
that needed to be born was already
gestating, all encompassed
in the letters that spell *Ave Maria*:
the love that shatters personality,
that ends up camping in an ox's stall.
I didn't look up to see it there,
the glittering, spinning,
Bethlehem star.

## The Car Salesman

She likes the fact that he can't find the car
on the lot or remember the price.
He's dejected, has had all the hopes
driven out of him. She likes that in a man.
He grew up looking for birds,
he tells her, can identify them now
just by the silhouette. In the morning,
he scouts out where the owls
will be, goes home for a cup of coffee,
then comes back later to find them.
He doesn't wear a ring.
She imagines taking him with her
to concerts at the Fine Arts Center,
would like to come in on his arm, surprise
her colleagues with her taste in men.
She would like to taste this man,
if only once, sit with him in a bar
drinking beers and laughing
at the Ford Corporation. She would like
to get drunk and dance with him
to the amateur band playing songs
of the seventies, or stay cool and sober
as a chalked cue, and win game after game
of pool, the men's quarters lined up
on the polished edge of the table.
After work, she'd sit beside him in his truck
and loosen his tie, loosen his laugh.
Sitting in his makeshift office, she feels
his depression, like the black hair that creeps
out of the neck of his shirt. She feels
the sadness of everything he's never dared
to want, doling out cars to those who can afford them
and those who can't. Now he's telling his wife
on the phone, "No, I don't want to, but I will,"
then making a note of that errand
he plans to forget. He's hearing the pull
of the tides on Cape Cod. "When I came here

in 1969, people couldn't understand
what I was saying. It was like I was talking
another language." He's still talking
his own language, the man who needs
to sell cars— "Just give me one more chance,"
he asks her on the phone—and whose heart
trails after birds. Sometimes it's so beautiful
what he sees when he's out in the woods,
he says, he feels inspired.
He thinks how he would write it down.
Then when he gets home, it's gone. Flown
like some bird he can't identify, flown
like something in his life he's been trying
to get a glimpse of, something he was sure
he'd recognize immediately, if he saw it,
just from the silhouette.

## Crazy Jane Meets a Bear

"I've been looking for you everywhere,"
she says when she finally meets him.
She has been chasing the bear, but the bear
is smart. He kneels down
to brush over his tracks with the soft
branch of a fir. He catches a hint
of her scent, and is gone. It's not
that he's afraid of Jane, he just
doesn't want to meet her by himself
in the woods. No one knows
what she might do, if provoked. She
has no fear of bears. She's always wanted
a dance partner taller than herself.
Sometimes she carries a bag of berries,
a slab of ham, to attract the bear,
preferably a grizzly. If she's going
to go to all this trouble, she wants
to find a big one. She knows
he could rip her apart with those strong hands,
knows he could lift and toss her
out of his path, but she's used
to the risk. She muses to herself,
"Can a girl propose?"
She decides not to stand
upon etiquette. He is afraid
she would embarrass him
if he introduced her to his friends.
She never did have much fashion sense.
"I am divorcing my husband and moving in
with a bear," she announces at a party.
Then she plunges her hand
into a pot of honey. "Some sweets
I reserve for him," she says,
licking her own fingers.

## The Driver

A dream that might explain why my lovers are sometimes women and sometimes men. But the dream doesn't care about the dreamer or what she feels a need to explain.

I read a story about a man who fell in love with a mannequin, bought her out of the store window, took her home and made love to her, spent quiet evenings communing with her, expressing his thoughts, noting her responses.

All was bliss for the man and mannequin until he began to suspect that the chauffeur was having an affair with his Helen. Because he could not endure the thought of her with another man, he killed her. That was end of the story.

But the dream has other plans.

Helen, the mannequin, has a good life. The man does all the cooking, makes her drinks, dresses her expensively, tucks her lovingly into bed. Still, something is missing.

She doesn't know what it is about the chauffeur, but in his presence, her painted skin begins to itch, she feels the prelude to a sneeze behind her cheekbones, her elbows start to crack, the arches of her feet relax. She feels heat, not from the man beside her, but her own.

She sends the chauffeur to warm up the car, then meets him at the door. "Move over," she says into his open window, "I'm driving."

## Crazy Jane Sleeps on Page C of the Logician's Dictionary

Crazy Jane wakes up feeling contumacious.
She's tired of listening to the birds'
contentious chatter. She knows they are spreading
rumors about her. How can she confute
their calumny? She learned once in school
about contradictions: The ball
is on the floor. The ball is not
on the floor. If one is true,
the other must be false.
If Jane slept last night
in her own bed, she did not sleep
in the priest's bed.
Or she could employ
logical contraries—
all of the following may be false:
there is a warm spot still in the priest's rumpled bed;
Crazy Jane has always loved the church;
Jane said her prayers last night
before climbing into her own bed.
However, if one of these statements is true,
the others must be false.
And who but Jane is to say
whether she remembered her prayers last night
and whether she whispered them
into a priest's ear?

## Expert

I'm going after a weedy sprout of a tree
with my shovel. A man who tried to kiss me
a few nights ago on my front porch walks by
with his dog. He tells me the tree's not an ash
but a Siberian elm, then pulls it out
expertly, wrapping the wiry stem around his hands
to get a better purchase. His life, he says, is in upheaval.
He's getting a divorce. I lean on the shovel.
He looks at my breasts. He says a line in French,
which I ask him to translate: *The heart*
*has its logic, which logic can't comprehend.*
But I'm not thinking about my heart.
I want him to wrap his hands around me
as if I were Siberian elm, and pull.

## Fireweed

The fireweed is first to grow
where the woods have been ravaged
by fire. Its tiny white tongues
dangle from the bells.
Sprung up among stumps,
flickering purple,
it is passion rekindled
waiting for something to burn.

## Crazy Jane: Nothing Personal

Most men want to sleep with me.
I try not to take it personally.
My skin smells like the outdoors
to them, crisp and raw. I move
like a beast moves—a bear, a deer
or an elk, antelope.
I try not to take it personally—
it has to do with their wives,
who smell like the involuntary perfume
stuck in the pages of magazines,
the kind you don't want
to sit next to on an airplane.
They love the fact
that I don't need them, don't look up
when they turn the doorknob
and enter, don't hold them
with the two fists of my eyes. Sometimes
they mistake me for mother nature,
or their own mothers, which they seem
to find erotic. They sense
I am something they can't
get their hands around, can't clamp
down, and so, to keep desire alive,
they desire me. They all look so young to me
and afraid, when they take
their pants down and the little animal,
ever hopeful, attentive, stands
on its hind legs. It's hard
to remain untouched
when you've slept with many men: I can't,
in truth, remember any of them
personally.

## Crazy Jane Defaults on Her Loan

Why did the man give her the money in the first place
if he wanted it back?

She thought he probably wanted
to have sex with her,
and that she could simply flirt
and refuse.

The man didn't mention about the money—
that he wanted it back.

She supposes if she had put it to bed in the bank
it would have multiplied, like grasshoppers,
but she made a house of her money
and now she can't rub the bills against each other
to see if they'll breed.

There is a big fire in the belly
of the house. It gestured to her
with its fiery hair,
did its dance, mocking her.

She knows it wants out of that
big unbreakable jelly jar.

She knows those flames are in there licking and fucking.
She would like to toss some dollars in
to appease the fire mouth.

She doesn't have any bills left.

When she was a child,
the only money she saw was coins.
She knew what they meant.

If she still had her money,
she would stitch her bills into a skirt
to wear to the town dance.

## She Keeps Her Heart

in a jar the way they do in the Biology building.
That way, whoever wants to break it
has to break the jar first.
Most of the time she doesn't need it with her
anyway.
Most of the time she feels lighter
without it.

When she was a girl, she had a red wagon.
Her heart's like that, something she can pull
with a handle, but hard to steer
if it gets going downhill.

In school, she liked dissection,
frogs, fetal pigs.

So she's given her heart to science—
and when she gets lonely, she goes
and folds her hands around the jar.

## The Visitation

Light touches the girl's uncovered breast
like a hand. She feels a stirring in her womb.
*I am among you now.* She thought
she'd find god *there,* in the church
gilt with ritual, the altar overflowing
with yellow, white, red gladiolus,
Christ serene on the cross.
She brings one hand to a breast.
She hadn't wanted to grow them.
She didn't mean to meet him like this,
in her own bedroom, her white confirmation dress
still hanging in the closet. Her mother tried
to tell her, sat with her in the dark school gym
while the film projector rolled and clicked.
Her mother's words sounded funny,
over-pronounced. She would have liked
to keep the words in that dark room, or rolled up
in a canister with the undeveloped film.

And where is her god now?
Has he written anything in that red ink?
He has not stamped the whorls of a new fingerprint,
pink of a baby's squinched face.
Why did he wake her that morning,
like a lover slipped in through the window
of her parents' house? Was there a message for her
in the strange inkblot, finger of her womb
starting to write on the still-white page?

# You Are Here

## I. The Map

I see birdprints, claw marks, something a seer
could read as an oracle. Pine trees
on a hillside. No water,
but a gene pool. Were we made
in the Garden of Eden
or configured in a double helix?
The shapes won't give themselves up.
How am I supposed to read what you have made?
Do you call this a map?—with no west or north,
only the blue dot marking *You are here*.

## II. The Bed

I see you've given me a boundary.
I am to stay within it.
When the man comes at night, offering me
his passionate DNA, I'll remain
a single helix along the bed's axis.
Out of my mouth, the *no*
of your creation.

## Total Immersion

Tonight she kissed me in the car,
my former lover, then went on talking.
I couldn't hear the words, and answered,
"I want to kiss you again."
She says she loves my touch,
that my hand melts her thigh—
then she's leaving, going to sleep
in her own bed.
                         All evening we listened
to blues in a bar. The musician, white,
was competent, her fingers
moved well, but she didn't slip
into the river of blues. My lover's afraid
to touch me in this bar, where,
in the hall outside the bathroom,
a cluster of men makes queer jokes.
She wears two rings,
one mine, one her new girlfriend's.
And me?
I too walk an unsteady line—
sit back in the booth, relaxed, a little happy
I can pass for straight. In the car outside,
we kiss, and I pray no one is nearby to see.
Earlier, standing in her kitchen,
I saw in the window next door
a woman undressing,
throwing one arm in the air
thrilling to her nakedness, one breast
showing itself to me across the way.
I am going to write poems that no one will like.
I will stand, like the woman
before her unshuttered window,
and reveal myself. And why?
Because my lover gets out of the car
and says goodnight. Because we are not
making love in her dark apartment.

Since I cannot entrust this body
into private hands, I offer it,
naked, in a poem.
                    Dear God,
take me into the stream,
let the water touch my skin like lovers' tongues,
let me be baptized in the current of my pulse,
immersed in the river that cuts its own course
through the stone of this world.

## The Mineral of Skin

I don't want to sleep
with Truth or Beauty, just want
the life that other women have,
the man's key inserted
between their legs, to open
their lives or lock them
in place.
          I am afraid
of leaving the path, afraid
of the sound the branches make
groaning to each other.

At home, I sleep with the light on.
Every night, I'm hungry.
I want salt, salt, salt.
I undress the crackers
in the cupboard, feel in the dark
for anything that will feed me.

For years I learned to starve
in a slow, calculated way. I can survive
without words. I have asked
the stream to stop speaking
to me.

I live in a house with cracks in it,
one so big you can see the sky.
God will move the earth,
if she must, to break a sealed box.

It is not given to me
to live in silence, to turn in bed
without a lover's touch, a woman's
breath wrapping itself around me
like the silk strands of a cocoon.

I will be safe but not in the way
I intended. My words are lights
that burn all night. Love,
if I allow it, will keep me awake,
feeding on salt,
the mineral of skin.

## II.

And if the body were not the Soul, what is the Soul?

—*Walt Whitman*

# Listening

You can keep a dead person's spirit with you for four years,
a Lakota healer says, but if you do, you must attend
to nothing else those years, then let the spirit go.
In my yard, a flicker pecks at the dried grass, flight compressed
into its tiny form. Once when my spirit tried to leave,
when I became too scared to live, Rose kept me with her.
She made me meals, put me to bed on her couch.
After she died, I kept looking for a sign—
the yellow flowers hatching in December,
a tiny rainbow that bloomed between clouds.
I saw someone at the movies last night who looked like Rose,
but younger, happy, motioning and mouthing something
to her lover who had just stepped inside.
The last time I saw Rose, I read to her.
She couldn't speak, but she opened her eyes
and spelled on the chart that looked like a Ouija board,
*I'm listening. I just like to close my eyes.*
It took so long to spell it out.
The woman in the movie theater is alive,
waving at her friend, forming words with her lips
but not saying them because she knows
he can't hear them across such a distance.

## The Silence

As a girl I twisted this tool into my mother's flesh.
I invented it myself, without examples,
and applied it in the places sensitive to pain.
Like carbon monoxide in a closed garage,
making the victim clutch and gasp, my method was ideal
for a woman whose mother punished her with silence,
who ignored her for days, making her words flap
like fish beached on ice—silence
that bullied her into a chair with a book
to voice the strict letters in her head.
I didn't know about her mother's silence.
She told me as we rode together
in the car. She talked and I drove,
my face stiff, as I cracked the window
for a little breeze, a little air.

## In *Arabic*

In her room in my house, a teenage girl speaks a language
I don't understand, a language she makes into gravel
to fling at her father, across a thousand miles.

Like a mood ring set on a stove, she changes
when she hears her father's voice—the atmosphere
around her turns dark purple, spiked

with yellow-green knives. He tells her to cover
her neck and head. When she argues,
it sounds as if she were being strangled,

scraping the bottom of a river whose current
presses her under. In Amman, women stream
the streets, heads scarved. A river can take a girl

and pin her to a rock, like an uncle pushing
a child against a wall, his hand bigger than the whole
of her sex. Some Arab women paint their hands

with intricate, hennaed patterns, like the swirls
this girl now doodles on the back of her fist
in blue pen, a design with four quadrants, a symmetry

with such confidence it must have arisen
from beneath her skin. She has her compass,
her knives. She will survive.

## Elegant

If I had to describe myself
in one word,
I think I'd choose *elegant*.
*Lesbian* is a word I wear
like a silk lining
that touches my skin
when I move. *Dyke*
is a set of charmed snakes
I sometimes wrap
around me.
I love women naked,
like water over sculpted rock,
like dunes that shift when I move
across them. Sometimes
I look in the mirror
and see my image reversed:
I'm short, with cropped hair, pants
worn low on my hips.
When I was thirteen I stopped eating
the family food: I made my own
and ate beside them. *Gay*
was a book I hid under my bed.
I slept with my body like a secret
lover. Once, I tried to kill her.
I thought I could step out
and leave her like a dress
pooled behind me on the floor.
Now, when I look in the mirror,
the one thing I can count on
is the scar, long and clean
and elegant.

## Crazy Jane Talks with Bones

Whenever she sees a bone she picks it up.
She has a room only for bones.
She likes the way skeletons are decorated,
with a dress of skin, the fringe of hair
on top, tiny moons growing out
at fingers and toes. Twenty moons
she wants to take in her mouth.
Crazy Jane knows she is going to die,
so she takes her skeleton out for walks
while she can. She knows it will be restless
in that nailed box.
When she becomes a spirit, she hopes
she'll be allowed to visit her skeleton,
sing it songs in its narrow cradle,
rock it the way she's seen mothers
rock babies. The skeleton may be glad
to lie down, to see her spirit approach
without the truckload of flesh
it always had to carry.
Always upright, poor spine,
poor skeleton. It grew more and more
rigid till it didn't want to bend.
She thinks her skeleton always wanted
to be like a tree, standing in a grove,
wind washing the bones,
making them sway and dance,
and nothing to support but the veined leaves
which sooner or later loosen their hold
and fly away like messages
to the solid, boneless earth.

## Pioneer

I want to see Mary Snow Sinton
step out of me and begin
sewing wrappers from her mother's
checked muslin dress. I want to hold
the implements she held, coffee grinder
heavy in her hand, fragrance snapping
out of the beans, want to lean
into the grater to tear the cheese
from its round, cheese that sat
in the coldhouse for months.
Of her brother, she says,
*maybe sorrow will ripen him.*
She doesn't know what's ahead for her,
two babies cold in her arms,
whom she'll prop up in the parlor
to pretend, for a few minutes,
that they live. She won't want to part
with their bodies. She doesn't know
how her heart will swell
around the kernals of sorrow,
two irritating grains that the heart makes
into pearls. I have her fingers
that can sew tiny stitches, gifts
for the children I might not have,
who might never live. She didn't think
of the losses that could ensue,
baby and baby gone to the grave,
another almost grown, gone.
What have I chosen—
no children, no family to gather
around the candles I provide?
Mary Snow Sinton steps out of me
with her tongs for canning, the jars
boiling, jumping in the rack.
The peaches, soft as babies' heads,
lie in piles in the sink.

## Radish

Summers my sisters and I pulled radishes,
seizing the greens, tearing the bulbs
up from the thread that held them
like the strand to my last bloody tooth.
We tossed them in loose bunches by the fence.

Tonight it's hot and you lie
uncovered. The thin light winds backwards
into sleep, and you are embryo,
curled in a pulsing dark.
I have never had children, never cut
the cord that sets them breathing
or listened, afraid
for the beating to stop.
Now, as I touch the quickness
in your side, trace the veins
that anchor your branching hands
to their stems, I understand
why the plant is fiercely green, why the red
vegetable clings in the crumbling dirt,
how easy to pluck
from its root the delicate heart.

## Crazy Jane Goes to Painting Class

*You can never paint the same stroke*
*twice.* All her paintings
look like crazy women. Their hair
stands on end. Their faces
are cracked. Electric waves
surround their bodies. They are
pink, orange, magenta, yellow, blue.
They don't look like Crazy Jane
but she sees them when she looks
in the mirror. She paints
the heart on the right hand side
because Crazy Jane has never
had her heart in the right place.
Inside the heart is a baby
in a cradle or a coffin,
it's hard to tell. Someone kneels
beside it. Tomorrow she'll paint
the tears. Or maybe
the baby will get up and play
outside the cradle. She always
had a hard time telling
whether they were dead
or just sleeping.

## Relativity

Our lives will not flash before our eyes.
Light travels the curved walls of time
like a train whistle that lowers
in pitch while diminishing.
But when the train doesn't swerve
at the turn, or a girl, sleepy, looking for
the bathroom door, falls between cars—the light
does not intensify. There is no inward curve, no
illumination.
             Her parents hope she didn't see,
didn't feel the bare rail, the clutch
of wheels. Still, they wish
they'd kissed her again, pressed
every bone to their hearts,
like a fern making a fossil in sand.

They store her suitcase
in an upstairs room, an atom, intact.
Below, the clock sounds like the clack of ties.
For those on board there is no
relativity: the shriek
of the whistle does not fade.

## Epithalamion

—for my sister Kathy, 1952-1961

On the train speeding toward Madrid, you and Marilyn
talked on your bunks, while I slept, a baby.
She asked if you were ever going to get married.

"Of course," you said, your life at nine still perfect,
and marriage another snapshot of you with your dazzling smile.
Now Marilyn has children older than you were

when you stepped off the train in the dark by accident—and I,
an adult, find nothing in marriage uncomplicated, nothing pure.
We imagine you living on, your life tracing its true course

without friction or gravity, while sadness tarnishes
the lives we pictured as children. All you can say is "Of course,"
as if all questions were direct, all answers simple.

Your face in the snapshots never changes, your smile never diluted
by doubt. Fear of death will never make you turn
to your lover in bed, to touch his body's astonishing warmth.

## Train

I catch only a glimpse
of the face I love, flickering
at the window, as I stand
in the weeds with my boxes.
If only we could stop the train
long enough to exchange our gifts,
who would mind the parting then,
embracing on the iron step,
holding each other's faces
still, for one minute—
then the whistle opens like a scream,
the wheels grab the rails,
and the body of white steam rises.

## Weeding the Cosmos
### —for my sister

I'm in the garden, pulling up cosmos
before the ground freezes,
enjoying the work, discerning,
among the many stems, which to seize
and take, which are entwined
with fledgling lupine. I tug
the sturdy stalks, shake dirt-packed
root balls, leaving chard and parsley,
late tomatoes.

I clear most of this patch of garden.
But I don't finish. I am wild inside
with anger now at this patient work. You, Kathy,
left everything undone. You made a mistake,
and now you can't do anything—
can't bring a man's flesh to life,
can't grow ovaries rich with eggs that leap
to meet the sperm, can't grow miraculously fat,
while the child forms fingernails and sprouts hair,
can't surrender so much to pain
that the baby bursts out of you, crying.

I don't either, waiting, as if for your
permission, or forgiveness.

This fall, in the weeks before the anniversary
of your death, all the people I love leave.
One friend finds a husband, one goes off to school.
Two boys I adore, both four years old,
move away. My lover travels to Europe
with another. A friend tells me
*be sweet to yourself, there are times like this*
*when you can't write,*
but I know it's an excuse. As you
are an excuse. You're dead.
It's done.

My life's my own.

# III.

Through my small, bonebound island I have learnt all I
know, experienced all, and sensed all. All I write is
inseparable from the island.

—Dylan Thomas

## Ocean

I had forgotten anemone,
unshelled flesh, lifting
and sighing in the rocking water.
You bring me back to ocean,
to a forest of pillars under a wharf,
a place as strange as the dreams I visit
each night in the drifting bed,
anchored to your brown body.
You peel a starfish from the piling,
let me touch the crust of skin,
secret mouth. We find a living
sand dollar and toss our wealth
back to the sea. In the dark
I make love to you,
your shifting sand
underneath me
still holding the day's heat.

## Joy

—for a friend who lives by the sea

I came to look for shells, but something pulled me
to a cove of rocks where mussels cluster, pointed
brown and white, and when I touched one it moved, alive.

As I turned toward the water, I felt grief returning,
my long familiar, and I thought about you
and the songs that sadness might sing in your body.

I grew up on the shores of a grief as large as the sea,
and I know her tides and colors. I know how to move with her
as skillfully as a surfer who makes love to a wave's changing shape.

And I know there is another sea, yours, where real surfers rise
on the joy of a wave, where last night I saw a green flame—
quick as a fuse where the water broke—ignite and disappear.

## Questions

She asks questions I can't answer—
*What kind of tree? What kind of church?*
*When does the spring*
*usually end?*

I love her in the morning, wild
as the cockatoo with the uncanny blue eye
who screams from the roof
of the neighbor's house.

The tree creaks
with the plums' weight.
*Is this the usual harvest?*
I shake the abundant branches,
fill my hands with this year's fruit.

## She

She, she said. *It's a she.*
Who moves like a seal,
her skin slippery, lips lovely.
Whose hair exuberates
when day comes, waving her dreams
against the blue. You
I'd dreamed of without knowing,
musical fingers, plucking strings,
musical thighs. The hidden
kiss. Maker of music
wherever she walks.
The doorways sing
as she passes through. *She,*
I say. *And me.*

## Crazy Jane: Alike in This

Crazy Jane has never worn gold lamé shoes
or thought of herself as someone's mistress.
She's never turned the word *artifice*
over in her head, or thought about the difference
between Latinate and Anglo-Saxon roots.
*Amphibrach* and *dactyl* mean nothing to her,
though branches tap rhythms on her windowpane.
Crazy Jane has never worn lipstick, never meant
to *seduce*, never confused that word
with *success*. She's never heard of *novelettes*—
her life is a single tree growing up through her body.

However, like me, she does sometimes wake up startled,
as if she'd bumped her head on the lid of her coffin.
Crazy Jane and I are alike in this:
in the grave, all odors of lovers convert to memory,
all words that issued with the breath, all titles, stigmas.
When our lives are engraved in stone,
neither Crazy Jane nor I will reside
under the rubric "Mother" or "Much Beloved."
Alive, we could never meet. But above our clay,
in fields gone to flowers, the same wind
will shake bracts and rattle anthers.

## Body Painting

At night he makes me his canvas. My nipples
become faces, my navel a ball tossed
between children. Then animals! A giraffe rooted
in my pelvis that twists its neck

to graze on the leaves of my spine,
a dog that sniffs at the nest of hair. Coyotes
howl on each shoulder. The paint
is thick as semen. How do I possess

these vibrant colors, confident geometries?
He follows the logic of color, knows that my arms
are yellow, shoulders purple, that a broad red stripe
proclaims the center of my back.

Like a dentist finding the right tool, he picks
the brush. Some fine and flexible, some fanlike,
asking his hand to arc. He knows the sensation of each,
and my skin answers, tickled, stroked.

Then I pull him toward me, not afraid of smearing.

## Train Whistle

I wake up to my lover on the phone,
singing his repertoire of train songs.
He does an impressive train whistle,
mixing it liberally into every song.
His favorite is the one his father made up,
about not using the bathroom
while the train is in the station.
It's set to the tune of the Minute Waltz,
and moves abruptly from toilet etiquette
to a conclusive "I love you."
I'm glad to be serenaded out of sleep,
humored into the day's happiness
by my exuberant lover, who might
be unhappy if he could manage
to care about what's past. I haul
my past with me like a freight train.
It's how I know that I am real:
when I pull forward, something resists.
But this morning I'm still in bed,
and my hips begin to sway,
my whole body humming
the way a train does
after the engine starts up,
and my lover, like an unruly
passenger, is singing his train songs
to get the day moving,
making his very impressive
whistle sound at every chance.

## Swaying

The woman reads in her hammock,
feet draped over the ropey edge,

balanced by the weight
in her bottom, hips,

hardly swinging
just hanging

suspended in green day
like a leaf in shady, luminous light.

It doesn't matter what she's reading;
she'll read something else next week

and will forget this book,
but her body will remember

the almost
imperceptible rocking,

the rest she found there,
her head supported, forgetting

everything outside the woods.
Grove of time in which all

is suspended, everything waits
till she turns the last page,

rolls slightly to the side,
swings her feet to the ground

and walks off
still in her book,

a pocket of green inside her now,
flowing green light resting and swaying.

## My Mother's Beauty

If I could recover my mother's beauty,
    look in the mirror and see her
        young face staring back, everything

could be different. I could unravel
    the past like a thread
        pulled out of a hem,

stitches popping, without breaking.
    I could roll the black and white film
        of romance and courtship back, back

to the scene where my mother
    doubles over with her roommate Gertie,
        laughing. She wasn't yet caught

in a photo, a story, the moving picture
    that towed her inexorably
        toward the happy ending.

If I could recover her beauty,
    I would hold it in my hands
        like precious water,

not scatter it over the sleeping
    form of a husband, three children
        who refuse to be still.

I want to flick back through all the frames
    that hold her face, want to burn
        the movie, the books

the whole story of love
    that takes a woman's beauty
        out of her hands, that takes

her motion away,
       saying, here, stand still,
              let me take your picture—

as if her life could ever stop flowing.

## The Moment

In those days, Betty Crocker
always called for sifted flour, and so
in homes across America, women sifted.
When my mother's mother turned
the wobbly red knob, hulls and stones
jumped in the wire basket,
but by my mother's time
the flour was fine—
now women sifted to achieve
precision, purity, perfection.
It made the white flour whiter.
Then flour came in bags,
already sifted, and women stopped
making their own cakes and bread,
and didn't have time anyway
for sifting. But for a flicker
of history, my mother stood
staring down the tin cylinder,
the moment shuttered
into tiny parts, slowed
by the fanning blunt blades—
nothing to do but watch
the perfection of time, falling
into the waiting bowl.

## Things to Do

All the lists I've made of things to do—
if I cut them into strips and rolled them up
like a ball of string, stood in my birthplace
and unraveled the ball, it would be longer,
much longer, than my life.

My house silent when I come home.
My sister's baby on the phone,
his breathing, his sucking sounds.

Lightning at tree line. I've never seen
the tiny flowers that thrive there.

I buy a new dress,
but clothes, too, grow old.

My aim is not good. I've been here
forty years and still can't knock down
bottles at a carnival, or throw a baseball
like a man.

Tomorrow: breakfast, swimming. No dogs.

I dreamed I was staying in a hotel room,
and when I looked in the closet, I found
clothes from all stages of my life,
none of them lost, none gone.

For each person who asks, I tear a leaf
from the tree of my body.

Some don't ask.
I tear leaves for them anyway.

Things to do later: write shocking poems,
wear mismatched patterns, rest
in my cradle of bones.

## Conception: Dialogues with Several Children and a Cosmologer

On her ninth birthday, Rachel tells me, "I used to think that God made people by drawing them on the wall and then bringing them to life with his magic powers."

"What do you think now?" I ask.

"Now I know about the *whole* process," she says with authority. "It's a very interesting process."

⁂

I watch the "Sunday Night Sex Show," hoping my seventeen-year-old niece Nazirah will come watch, to learn about sex. She sits down for a few minutes, long enough to explain to me what a female condom is.

⁂

Rachel says, "Ummm. . . what do you call that thing that a man puts on his—mmmmm—so you don't get pregnant?"

⁂

Her Muslim family expects Nazirah to wear the scarf and long sleeves, to be home every night by dark. She wears transparent shirts over dark bras, buys a banner for the windshield of her white sports car that reads, "Diva." She slips out at night to drive to her boyfriend's house.

⁂

I take Eli to the hospital to see his new baby brother. His mother has had four children with three different boyfriends. Leaving the Catholic hospital, Eli spots a marble sculpture of the Virgin Mary and child. "Look!" he says, excited, pointing at the Virgin, "a girlfriend!"

⁂

My lover is a cosmologer. "There is some strange dark matter that we can not see or detect," he explains. "At least ninety percent of matter that should be visible is missing."

✍

Eli spreads a measuring tape across the expanse of table and scrutinizes numbers on the stiff yellow band. "Table, eight inches," he announces. "Shoe, 'leven inches." He holds his tape up to a large sculpted female nude. "Girlfriend, two inches."

✍

Nazirah talks on the phone with her best friend, who is explaining Christianity. She hangs up and says, "I don't believe any of that stuff about God having kids."

✍

Eli's mother is in jail and he is sent to stay with strangers. On the phone, he says, "I have a scream in my mouth but I can't get it out."

✍

"Your hand," my lover says, "is made of stellar debris from fierce primeval fires."

✍

Eli says, "If I put a marble in my mouth, the scream gets really quiet."

✍

My lover writes, "It is almost certain now that the cosmos was made by an intelligent mind that designed it for life. It could not just have 'happened.'"

⚬⚬⚬

"If my mother don't pick me up," asks Eli, "will you come pick me up? Do you know where I am at?"

⚬⚬⚬

Christopher, age six, stops to look at the chalk drawing we're making on the sidewalk.

"We forgot something!" he says.

"What?" I ask.

"Where God lives." He draws a blue line of sky. "There," he says. "God has to show."

# Hush

—for Tom Mauch

You have to be quiet to see it.

The peacock hears your step
on pine needles. Turns his head.

You have to be as quiet as a chapel
where monks are breathing.

You have to be as still as a vase of flowers,
engraved with solemn letters.

Quiet as peacock feathers touching.

Hush, watch, be still.

You touch the delicate flowers.
You place water around their feet.
Yours are the enormous mulched pumpkins.

You have been knocking at the wrong door,
lamenting the lost key to the secret garden,
but you are in paradise. The grass is mown,
flowers are purple in bloom, pumpkins
sit in their nests, raspberries
loosen themselves from their thorny thumbs
to drop into your bucket.
This arch of slatted white wood
leads to the greenest place.
Your hand wipes mud
from the pumpkins. Hush.

Mild air after harsh

Touching skin

You can hardly hear the river

It's the sound of the earth turning
It's that slow
It's that old

It's a silence this side of deafness

It has never heard a clock

It is the quiet at the eye
of each peacock feather

watching watching watching


I can touch it

Pumpkins and raspberries

The gate is open

Quiet

Not like the grave

A quiet with breath in it
Breathing

## Blizzard

I'd allowed myself to thirst and thirst,
and when I drank
from the cup of her body,

the snow began to fall
in flakes as big as feathers,
hushing the streets, covering cars.

It drew neighbors out
to push snow from one another's trees
where branches hung loaded,

and the limbs, suddenly freed,
sprung toward sky.
Others heaved, cracked, and fell,

as if from grief's unbearable weight.
My neighbor leapt across my lawn
to check the chimney, so that fumes

wouldn't kill me. Perhaps I will die,
now that I have sung her shape,
now that I have tasted fruit so sweet

it makes me want to save even the smallest
branch of peach and plum,
fruit that drives me into the world

with my shovel and too-small gloves,
as snow lands on my hair,
in my eyes, on my wrists exposed

below the coat, snow that soon
will melt into earth, replenishing
the cup of her body.

## Sand

I have a tone inside me
that has not been sounded. Or only once
or twice. Once she went straight to the center
of me, once she could have walked through me
like a tunnel. She could have seen sky
on the other side of me.
I could have washed my hands in sand,
then touched her, turned her to sand.
I'm the opposite of Midas: I want to touch
what's returning to earth.

## We Say

There's a river that flows
underneath all things:
in *that* river I will swim.

I slide in as if I were one of the turtles,
a lucky one, not flattened on the road.
Will god speak to me?
What sits at the center and mocks?
What sits at the center and beckons?

Only the holy ponds are bottomless—
a steam lifts off the water:
I and I, evaporating.

## Biographical Note

Jane Hilberry's first poetry teacher was her father, poet Conrad Hilberry, who sensed her interest in writing when she was a teenager. They spent many evenings at the kitchen table, exchanging work or discussing poems he was to teach the next day.

Hilberry graduated Phi Beta Kappa from Oberlin College, worked in the Publications Department of the Denver Art Museum, and continued her education at Indiana University, where she received an M.A. in Creative Writing and a Ph.D. in Medieval and Renaissance literature. She was one of the first editors of *The Indiana Review*.

Hilberry now teaches literature and Creative Writing at Colorado College in Colorado Springs, where, for the past sixteen years, she has developed methods to cultivate students' creativity. She has recently published and taught workshops in the United States and Canada on the subject of Creativity and Leadership. Interested in visual art as well as poetry, she has published a book of art criticism/biography titled *The Erotic Art of Edgar Britton* (Ocean View Books, 2001). She has also published two chapbooks of poems.

Her honors include the Colorado Council on the Arts Recognition Award for Poetry and a Colorado Endowment for the Humanities Research Award.